Put each word into the correct senten

CW01665293

independent **ancient** **haul** **sockets** **exposed**
plink-plonked **stubborn** **lurked** **gaping** **numb**

Mum lifted the duvet and .... the hidden sweets.

The ice lolly made my tongue ....

We had to .... the boat over the sand.

Emily .... tunelessly on the piano.

That joke is .... – everybody's heard it already!

My .... sister would not tidy her room.

We had to work alone for the .... writing task.

Ronnie knew that a monster .... under his bed.

The cricket ball left a .... hole in the window.

Your eye .... protect your eye balls.

Read pages 3 to 11 of *Mary Anning: The Girl Who Cracked Open the World*. Record your thoughts about each of the three questions in the spaces below.

The looking question is …
How does Mary find fossils?

The clue question is …
How does Mary feel about being a fossil hunter?

The thinking question is …
Why do some people find fossils interesting?

Do you have any questions? Write them here.

Think about the conversations you have had about this text. What more have you learned? Complete the activity below.

Describe Mary and explain how she is different from other girls in the town.

Imagine a conversation between Joseph and Mary after they've found the enormous fossil. Write the conversation in the spaces below.

Joseph

Mary

Joseph

Mary

Feedback

Look at the words and phrases. What do you think they mean? Write your notes in the spaces below.

paddles

My Notes

inside out

My Notes

curious

My Notes

Draw lines to match the bold word in each sentence to the word or phrase which is closest in meaning. Look up any words you don't know in a dictionary.

The doctor **examined** my ears.

The children were **curious** about the new people next door.

An owl **expert** visited the school to teach us about barn owls.

The **ancient** building was falling down.

A strange **creature** with an orange tail came out of the woods.

The children queued up **eagerly** for their party bags.

I am **convinced** that there is a monster in my cupboard.

- enthusiastically
- wondering and asking questions
- certain
- specialist
- closely looked at
- extremely old
- animal

Read pages 12 to 21. Record your thoughts about each of the three questions in the spaces below.

The looking question is ...
What did Mary do with the fish?

The clue question is ...
Was Henry de la Beche a good friend to Mary?

The thinking question is ...
What did the other scientists think of Mary?

Do you have any questions? Write them here.

Think about the conversations you have had about this text. What more have you learned? Complete the activity below.

Describe the different ways in which Mary is a good scientist. Draw and list the different things she does.

Imagine you are interviewing Mary about the fossils she has found. What questions would you ask? Write your questions on the clipboard below.

Feedback

Look at the words below. Do you know what they mean? Record your thoughts about the meanings, then look each word up in a dictionary.

I think this word means ...		The definition in the dictionary is ...
	geology	
	palaeontology	
	Europe	

Use the bold words to write your own sentences in the spaces provided.

I **tucked** my shirt in and put on my jumper.

We made many **discoveries** when we were looking for my shoes.

John had his leg put in **plaster** when he broke it playing hockey.

The coal train had 20 **wagons** and took a long time to go past.

Read from page 22 to the end of the book. Record your thoughts about each of the three questions in the spaces below.

The looking question is ...
What did the third fossil look like?

The clue question is ...
How do we know that Mary is now famous?

The thinking question is ...
Was Mary lucky in her life?

Do you have any questions? Write them here.

Think about the conversations you have had about this text. What more have you learned? Complete the activities below.

Explain the title of the book.
How did Mary "crack open the world"?

Explain why Mary Anning is still remembered.

Discuss why Mary was not allowed to join the Geological Society.

Think about times when Mary has been lucky, unlucky, or has made her own luck. Write examples of each in the boxes below.

lucky

I think Mary is lucky because …

unlucky

I think Mary is unlucky because …

makes her own luck

I think Mary makes her own luck because …

Feedback

Look at the pictures and the words, then look up the words in the dictionary. What do you think they mean? Write your answers in the spaces.

My Notes

My Notes

My Notes

Look at the words below. Do you know what they mean? Record your thoughts about the meanings, then look each word up in a dictionary.

I think this word means ...		The definition in the dictionary is ...
	theory	
	evidence	
	roamed	

Read up to page 11 of *Death of the Dinosaurs*. Record your thoughts about each of the three questions in the spaces below.

The looking question is …
How might a meteor have killed the dinosaurs?

The clue question is …
Why is the layer of iridium interesting to scientists?

The thinking question is …
Why didn't all life on Earth die when the meteor hit?

Do you have any questions? Write them here.

Think about the conversations you have had about this text. What more have you learned? Complete the activities below.

Discuss whether the dinosaurs starved to death or died from the cold.

Describe other evidence for the meteor strike.

Describe what you think life on Earth was like once the dust cleared and the sun shone again.

What were the consequences of each event in the text? Write your answers in the spaces provided.

Dinosaurs had no natural predators.

Consequence ...

A meteor struck Earth.

Consequence ...

Feedback

Explore the focus word by completing the activities below.

Look up the focus word in a dictionary and write a definition.

Make up a sentence using the focus word.

continent

Draw a picture which shows the meaning of the focus word.

Use the bold words to write your own sentences in the spaces provided.

We went to **support** Alice when she ran the marathon.

My brother only **appeared** after the washing up was finished.

Before cars **existed** children had to walk to school.

Mr Canning **erupted** when the children kept talking.

Read the rest of the book. Record your thoughts about each of the three questions in the spaces below.

The looking question is ...
What happened to Pangaea?

The clue question is ...
Why did the change in the weather kill the dinosaurs?

The thinking question is ...
What would life on Earth be like if the dinosaurs had not died out?

Do you have any questions? Write them here.

Think about the conversations you have had about this text. What more have you learned? Complete the activities below.

How do we know the continents are still moving?

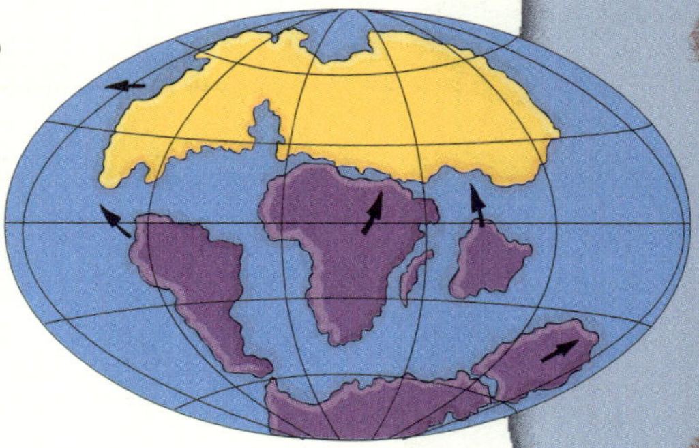

What did the dinosaurs need to survive?

What do you think killed the dinosaurs?

What would you say to the expert who supports The Great Disaster Theory? Tell them why you agree or disagree with them.

Feedback

Look at the pictures and the words, then look up the words in the dictionary. What do you think they mean? Write your answers in the spaces.

cart

My Notes

My Notes

thatched

pump

My Notes

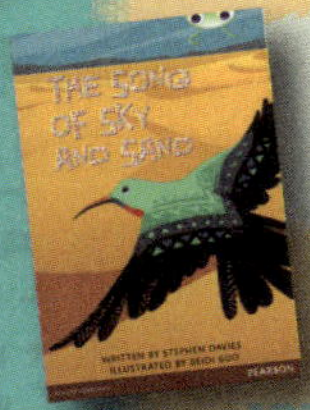

Put each word into the correct sentence.

shimmering perched pump pounding gazed narrowed shrugged overuse sprout

She .... on the top of the fence.

They had to .... water from the ground.

The trees had started to .... leaves.

He .... at the cows in the field.

She .... her shoulders.

The spade was broken from ....

The lane .... as they reached the house.

She was .... the grain with a stick.

They walked all day in the .... heat.

Read the first chapter of *The Song of Sky and Sand*. Record your thoughts about each of the three questions in the spaces below.

The looking question is ...
In which country is this story set?

The clue question is ...
Why had the water pump been overused?

The thinking question is ...
Is it right that the children should have to travel so far to get water?

Do you have any questions? Write them here.

Think about the conversations you have had about this text. What more have you learned? Complete the activities below.

Describe what you know about the setting now.

Explain how Ramata's life is different from your own.

Explain why it is a problem that the water pump was broken.

Think about what Ramata says to the donkey. Complete the activities below.

How do you think Ramata will keep her promise to the donkey?

How do you think the donkey is feeling?

Feedback

Look at the pictures and the words, then look up the words in the dictionary. What do you think they mean? Write your answers in the spaces.

mosquito net

My Notes

My Notes

acacia tree

well

My Notes

Use the bold words to write your own sentences in the spaces provided.

We went out into the **yard** to kick the ball around before dinner.

The two **elderly** women sat on the bench in the sunshine.

The children **shuffled** up to make room for Daisy.

Everyone jumped when someone started **pounding** on the door.

Read chapter 2. Record your thoughts about each of the three questions in the spaces below.

The looking question is ...
How did people drink during a drought in the past?

The clue question is ...
Why is Grandma not scared?

The thinking question is ...
Why doesn't Ramata's family move to the city?

Do you have any questions? Write them here.

Think about the conversations you have had about this text. What more have you learned? Complete the activity below.

Here is Ramata's family sitting around the fire. What do you think Ramata is thinking? What do you think she likes to do for fun?

Likes to do:

Thinks:

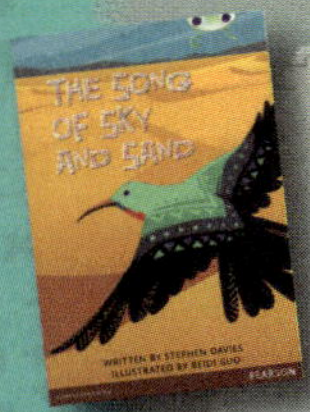

Ramata has started at your school. Write Ramata's letter home to Grandma. Remember to say how her life has changed, what she likes and what she doesn't like.

Grandma Bagayogo
Simbi
Mali

Feedback

Change each word so that it fits in the sentences.

impatiently

"Thank you for waiting .... for me."

"Don't be so ....! It's not your turn yet."

"Please be .... and don't rush me."

scowled

Janet sulked with a nasty .... on her face.

.... at the referee, Ben stormed off the pitch.

Matilda .... when she loses the game.

muttered

"I don't want to hear anybody .... as they line up."

"Don't .... ! Speak clearly!

Paul .... the answers quietly to Tamsin.

Draw lines to match the bold word in each sentence to the word or phrase which is closest in meaning. Look up any words you don't know in a dictionary.

The answer to the **riddle** was "teeth".

Last year's crops died because of the **drought**.

The Sun rises in the **East** and sets in the West.

The traveller **wearily** trudged along the road.

Jacob **seized** his coat and ran for the bus.

The sun sank below the **horizon** and the sunset was over.

The **constellation** of Orion is supposed to look like a man.

Simret was clearly **visible** as she hid behind the tree.

- showing
- lack of rain
- in a tired way
- the point where sky and planet meet
- grabbed
- puzzle
- towards the morning sun
- pattern of stars

Read chapter 3. Record your thoughts about each of the three questions in the spaces below.

The looking question is ...
What was the riddle about?

The clue question is ...
Why did Ramata wake up so early?

The thinking question is ...
Why do people see patterns in the stars?

Do you have any questions? Write them here.

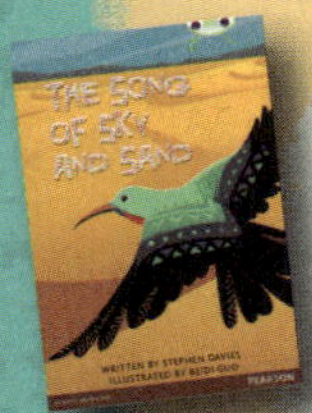

Think about the conversations you have had about this text. What more have you learned? Complete the activities below.

Why do you think that the information is put in a riddle?

Explain Ramata's connection with the earth and stars.

Explore different methods people use to find their way.

What has happened in the story so far? Use the flowchart below to summarise the main points.

1

2

3

4

5

6

Feedback

Look at the words below. Do you know what they mean? Record your thoughts about the meanings, then look each word up in a dictionary.

I think this word means ...		The definition in the dictionary is ...
	quest	
	loomed	
	swigs	

Use the bold words to write your own sentences in the spaces provided.

Roger **suspected** that the Moon was not in fact made of cheese.

The princess **insisted** that the crusts were cut off her sandwiches.

The girls **trudged** home in the rain.

Cinderella polished the floor until there wasn't a **speck** of dirt to be seen.

Read chapter 4. Record your thoughts about each of the three questions in the spaces below.

The looking question is ...
How does Grandma help them on their journey?

The clue question is ...
What dangers do the travellers face?

The thinking question is ...
Were the adults right to let the children go on the quest?

Do you have any questions? Write them here.

Think about the conversations you have had about this text. What more have you learned? Complete the activities below.

Explain how Ramata, Yusuf and Grandma are a good team.

Speculate why Ramata feels it's her job to find water.

Justify why the villagers sent the party with the last of the water.

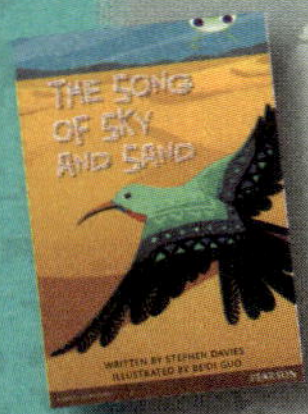

Imagine you are Ramata or Yusuf in the desert. What can you smell, touch, hear, taste and see? Draw or write your answers in the spaces below.

I can see ...

I can taste ...

I can hear ...

I can smell ...

I can touch ...

Feedback

Put each word into the correct sentence.

screeching	hoisted	slumped	exhausted
transfixed	emerging	gulped	enthralled

Benji was .... at the end of the race.

The bored children .... over their desks.

The .... owl swooped through the woods.

The audience was .... by the wonderful dancing.

"I thought I'd never find my way out!" cried Dad .... at last from the maze.

Alice had a stomach ache after she had .... down her lunch too quickly.

The children were .... by Grandpa's ghost stories.

The girl playing Tinkerbell was .... up to the ceiling to fly around the stage.

Explore the focus word by completing the activities below.

Look up the focus word in a dictionary and write a definition.

Make up a sentence using the focus word.

crevice

Write a word or phrase that means the same as the focus word.

Draw a picture that shows the focus word.

Read chapters 5 and 6. Record your thoughts about each of the three questions in the spaces below.

The looking question is ...
What is the crooked hand?

The clue question is ...
What does the sunbird tell them?

The thinking question is ...
Are the villagers' problems solved forever?

Do you have any questions? Write them here.

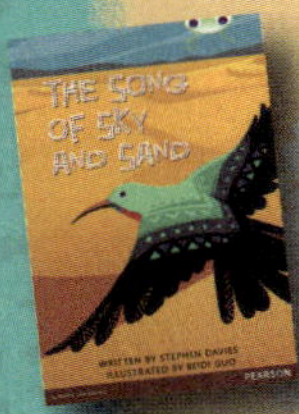

Think about the conversations you have had about this text. What more have you learned? Complete the activities below.

Explain the riddle in your own words.

Argue that Ramata and Yusuf should remember the old ways.

Imagine that you are the leader of the village of Simbi. Who will you let use the water and why?

In the space below, draw a map to show the journey that Ramata, Yusuf and Grandma went on from Simbi to the spring. Label each point and say what happened there.

Feedback

Reading Goals

This term I aim to ...

Find a new author I like!

Read a play
with friends!

Read the book of
my favourite film!

Learn a poem by heart!

Group Discussion Rules

- We will listen carefully to the person who is speaking
- Everyone should have a chance to speak
- We will give reasons for our ideas
- We can ask others for reasons if they don't say them
- **We can agree and disagree politely with each other**
- We will respect each other's ideas and opinions
- We will share all the information in the group
- We will try to reach an agreement together if we can

Add any other group discussion rules your class or group has decided on here:

- ....
- ....
- ....
- ....
- ....

Reading Tracker

Book title: ....

Author: ....

Date finished: .... Score out of 10 ☐

Book title: ....

Author: ....

Date finished: .... Score out of 10 ☐

Book title: ....

Author: ....

Date finished: .... Score out of 10 ☐

Book title: ....

Author: ....

Date finished: .... Score out of 10 ☐

Book title: ....

Author: ....

Date finished: .... Score out of 10 ☐

Book title: ....

Author: ....

Date finished: .... Score out of 10 ☐

Book title: ....

Author: ....

Date finished: .... Score out of 10 ☐

Book title: ....

Author: ....

Date finished: .... Score out of 10 ☐

Book title: ....

Author: ....

Date finished: .... Score out of 10 ☐

Book title: ....

Author: ....

Date finished: .... Score out of 10 ☐

Read-alikes

If you liked *Mary Anning*,
why not try ...

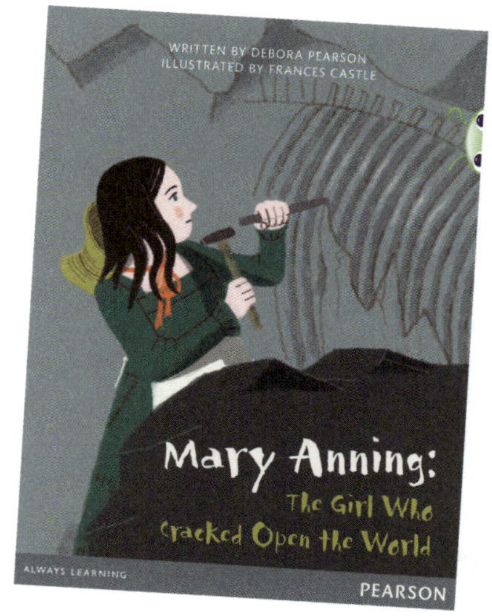

The Comic Strip Book of Dinosaurs
by Sally Kindberg and Tracey Turner

What Mr Darwin Saw
by Mick Manning and Brita Grandström

If you liked *The Death of the Dinosaurs*,
why not try ...

Boy, Were We Wrong About Dinosaurs
by Kathleen V. Kudlinski

Jurassic World Dinosaur Field Guide
by Thomas R. Holtz and Michael Brett-Surman

If you liked *The Song of Sky and Sand*,
why not try ...

The Fastest Boy in the World
by Elizabeth Laird

The Leopard Boy
by Julia Johnson

The types of text I have read this term

- Funny story ☐
- MYTH ☐
- FANTASY STORY ☐
- JOKE book ☐
- Scary story ☐
- Story set in another country ☐
- Story set a long time ago ☐
- Newspaper article ☐
- Poetry book ☐
- Book of facts ☐
- Magazine ☐
- Fairy tale ☐
- Play script ☐
- Science fiction story ☐
- Picture book ☐
- Comic ☐

Something else? Write it here:

....

The best new words I have learned this term

Word	What it means
palaeontology	The study of fossils

The best jokes I have read this term

What has a long neck, paddle-shaped legs and sixteen wheels?

A plesiosaur on roller skates!

Reading Record

Fill in these sheets for one story you have chosen yourself.

At the beginning

Title:

Author:

Why did you choose this book?

What score do you think you'll give it? /10

Who is the character you like most?

Has anything like this ever happened to you?

What questions do you have about the story?

What do you think will happen at the end?

At the end

Were your predictions right?

Is there anything that still puzzles you?

What score would you give this book? /10

Who do you think would enjoy this book?

The best facts I have read this term

Best Fact

There was once a time when all the continents were pressed together in one great mass of land called Pangaea.

Best Fact

Best Fact

Best Fact

Best Fact

Recommended Reads for Me

Think about someone in your group, class or family. What books would you recommend for them?

Recommended Reads for

....

A story I think they'll like:

A non-fiction book I think they'll like:

A poem I think they'll like:

An author I think they'll like:

What books have been recommended for you? Write them here.

Bug Club Comprehension is a fresh new approach that helps every child master comprehension. It uses a powerful and proven talk-based, mastery approach to help children develop a deeper understanding of texts.

Part of the Bug Club Comprehension programme, the workbooks provide:

- activities for each day of the teaching cycle
- clear, child-friendly designs that complement the accompanying texts
- formative assessment opportunities
- a 'Reading Journal' section for children to record their independent reading.

Series Consultants:
Wayne Tennent and David Reedy
Workbook and Teaching Card Authors:
Catherine Casey, Sarah Snashall and Andy Taylor

Published by Pearson Education Limited, 80 Strand, London, WC2R 0RL.

www.pearsonschools.co.uk

Designed by Karen Awadzi, Red Giraffe

Illustrated by Rachael Saunders, Andrea Castellani

First published 2016

20 19 18 17 16
10 9 8 7 6 5 4 3 2 1

British Library Cataloguing in Publication Data
A catalogue record for this book is available from the British Library

ISBN 978 0 435 18087 4

Printed in the UK by Ashford Colour Press.

Acknowledgements
The author and publisher would like to thank the following individuals and organisations for permission to reproduce photographs:

(Key: b-bottom; c-centre; l-left; r-right; t-top)

2 Alamy Images: MERVYN REES (b/MA). Shutterstock.com: abimages (c/MA)
15 Alamy Images: The Natural History Museum (MA)
17 Alamy Images: artpartner-images.com (DOD)
20 Science Photo Library Ltd: DIRK WIERSMA (DOD)
57 Shutterstock.com: Robbi (RJ)
62 Shutterstock.com: Robbi (RJ)

All other images © Pearson Education

www.pearsonschools.co.uk
enquiries@pearson.com

ISBN 978-0-435-18087-4